STICKMEN'S GUIDE TO YOUR BRILLIANT BRAIN

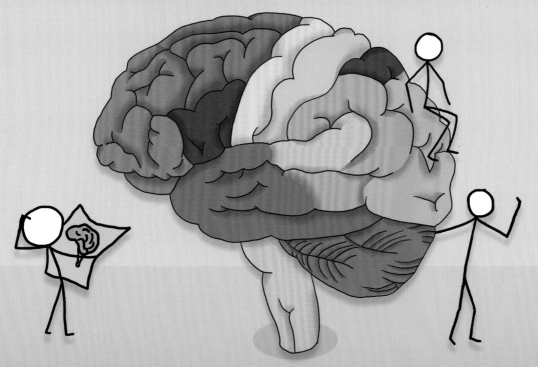

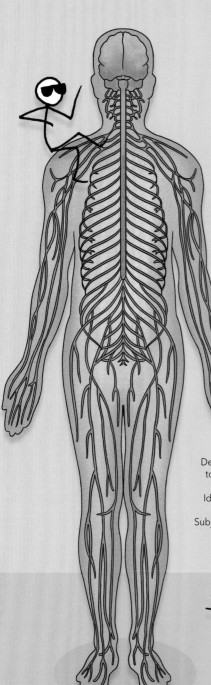

Thanks to the creative team:
Senior Editor: Alice Peebles
Fact Checking: Kate Mitchell
Design: www.collaborate.agency

Hungry Tomato®
A division of Lerner Publishing Group, Inc.
241 First Avenue North
Minneapolis, MN 55401 USA

For reading levels and more information, look up this title at
www.lernerbooks.com.

Main body text set in Avenir Next Medium 9.5/12.
Typeface provided by Linotype AG

Library of Congress Cataloging-in-Publication Data

Names: Farndon, John, author. | Dean, Venitia, 1976- illustrator.
Title: Stickmen's guide to your brilliant brain / John Farndon ;
illustrated by Venitia Dean.
Other titles: Your brilliant brain
Description: Minneapolis : Hungry Tomato, [2017] | Series: Stickmen's guides
to your awesome body | Audience: Ages 8-12. | Audience: Grades 4 to 6.
|Includes index.
Identifiers: LCCN 2016046945 (print) | LCCN 2016050332 (ebook) | ISBN
9781512432138 (lb : alk. paper) | ISBN 9781512450125 (eb pdf)
Subjects: LCSH: Brain—Juvenile literature. | Central nervous system—Juvenile
literature. | Senses and sensation—Juvenile literature.
Classification: LCC QP376 .F3575 2017 (print) | LCC
QP376 (ebook) | DDC 612.8/2—dc23

LC record available at https://lccn.loc.gov/2016046945

Manufactured in the United States of America
1-41768-23529-1/12/2017

STICKMEN'S GUIDE TO YOUR BRILLIANT BRAIN

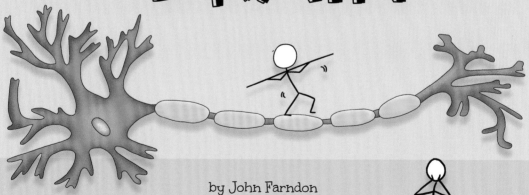

by John Farndon

Illustrated by Venitia Dean

HUNGRY
TOMATO®

Minneapolis

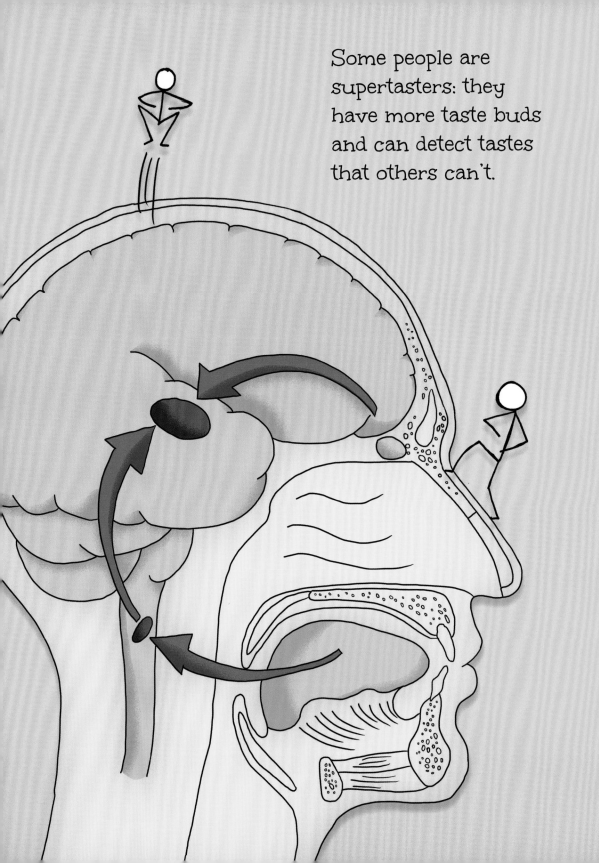

Some people are supertasters: they have more taste buds and can detect tastes that others can't.

Contents

Introduction   6

Central Control   8

You've Got a Nerve   10

Brainy   12

Inside Your Brain   14

Brain Map   16

Moving and Feeling   18

Seeing Things   20

Hear, Hear   22

Smell That, Taste That   24

Remember, Remember   26

The History of the Brain   28

More Brainy Facts   30

Index   32

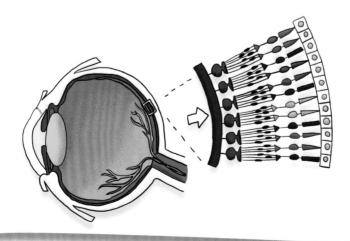

Introduction

Every creature has a brain, but we humans have especially clever ones. The human brain is a living supercomputer! But like a computer, it needs inputs and outputs, and that's where nerves come in. Nerves provide input by sending signals to the brain from sensors all over the body, and output by sending signals to tell the body what to do. Your brain and nerves make up the nervous system.

Brainy Neanderthals

We humans like to think we've got big brains. But Neanderthal people had even bigger brains. Neanderthal people lived 160,000 to 40,000 years ago in Eurasia. Their brains were about 30 percent bigger than ours. But an elephant has a brain three times as big as ours!

Intelligence Quotient

An Intelligence Quotient (IQ) test features a series of questions designed to test your brainpower. Most people get an IQ score between 85 and 115. Some very clever people get higher scores. But IQ scores don't really show how clever you are. They only show how good at IQ tests you are. The more you practice, the better you do!

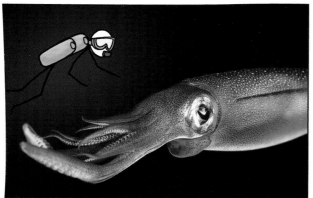

Just Squidding

Most nerves are far too small too see, except under a powerful microscope. But the squid has a nerve with an axon (tail) that is over 0.04 inches (1 millimeter) thick—thicker than cotton thread. The axon sends the signal that fires the squid's jet propulsion system—the jet of water it shoots out to give it a quick burst of speed. Scientists have learned a lot about how human nerves work by studying the squid's giant nerve.

Mind Your Brain

Scientists and other thinkers often argue about whether you think with your brain or your mind. Your brain is the mass of nerves inside your head that does your thinking. Your mind is all your thoughts. If your brain were a computer, your mind would be all the things a computer does.

Sigmund Freud, the world's best known psychologist

Brain Science

Different sciences involve different aspects of the brain and how it works. Neuroscientists study how the brain and nerves work physically. Cognitive neuroscientists study how the nerves in your brain make you think. Psychologists study people's minds and how they behave.

Central Control

Your nervous system is like a busy Internet, wired to every part of your body and whizzing messages back and forth. It's a two-way system. Sensory nerves send signals in toward the brain from sense receptors all around the body, such as the touch sensors in the skin. Motor nerves send signals in the other direction, out from the brain, telling the muscles to move.

Branching Out

The core of the nervous system is the brain and the bundle of nerves known as the spinal cord that runs down through the backbone. Together, the brain and spinal cord are known as the central nervous system *(shown in green)*. From this system, nerves branch out to the whole body through what is called the peripheral nervous system *(shown in pink)*. The main branches of the peripheral nervous system are the twelve pairs of cranial nerves (in the brain) and the thirty-one pairs of spinal nerves. All other nerves branch off these.

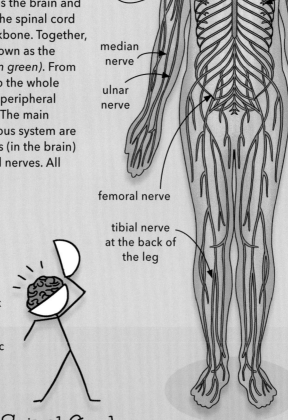

brain

spinal cord

intercostal nerves

radial nerve in the back of the arm

median nerve

ulnar nerve

femoral nerve

tibial nerve at the back of the leg

eight cervical nerves in the neck

twelve thoracic nerves in the upper back

five lumbar nerves in the lower back

six sacral nerves at the base of the spine

Spinal Cord

The spinal cord is the highway that carries all nerve signals to and from the brain. It is protected by cerebrospinal fluid. The thirty-one pairs of major nerves that branch off the spinal cord form four groups: the cervical, thoracic, lumbar, and sacral nerves.

Automatic Nerves

Along with the central and peripheral systems, you have a third system, the autonomic nervous system. This system controls automatic tasks such as heartbeat and digestion. It has two parts: the parasympathetic, which deals with everyday tasks; and the sympathetic, which prepares your body for action if you are ever in danger.

Fight or Flight

The autonomic nervous system gets your body ready for action in times of danger when you have to stand and fight or run away: the "fight or flight" reflex.

The Wandering Nerve

The vagus nerve gets its name from the Latin for "wandering"—and that's just what it does. It wanders all the way down from the base of your brain to your gut. On its way, it controls lots of things, from your breathing and heartbeat to the way you digest food.

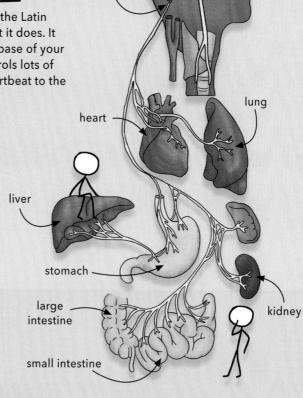

vagus nerve

lung

heart

liver

sciatic nerve

stomach

large intestine

kidney

small intestine

Sciatic Nerve

The sciatic nerve is the largest single nerve in your body. It runs down from your lower spine into your buttocks and thighs, then all the way down to your feet. It plays an important role in linking the spinal cord to the muscles in your legs and feet. It can sometimes cause a pain known as sciatica.

You've Got a Nerve

Your nervous system is made of lots of nerve cells strung together. Nerve cells, known as neurons, are unusual cells. While most cells are like little packets, neurons are a spidery shape with threads branching out in all directions to connect with other nerves, sense organs, or muscles.

A Nerve Cell

Nerve signals enter a neuron through any one of a bunch of spidery threads called dendrites. They then pass through the cell's nucleus and out the other side through a long tail, or axon, to connect to other neurons. Axons from several cells bunch together like threads in a string to make nerve fibers.

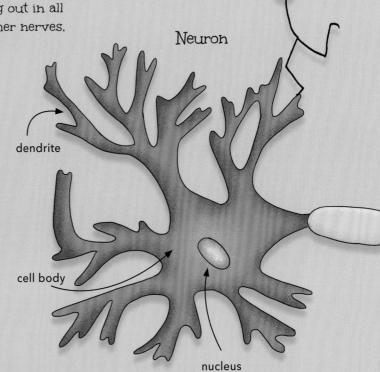

Neuron

dendrite

cell body

nucleus

How Nerve Signals Move

Nerve signals are sent with a mix of chemistry and electricity. When a nerve is resting, there are lots of little particles with negative electricity on the inside. Nerve signals start by opening "gates" in the nerve walls. This lets positive particles in. The positive particles are attracted toward the negative particles farther up the nerve.

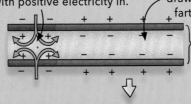

1. A nerve signal starts as gates open to let particles with positive electricity in.

Positive particles are drawn to negative ones farther up the nerve.

segment of axon

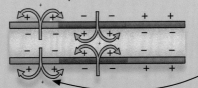

2. The signal sweeps up the nerve, as more gates open farther up to let particles in.

Other gates close behind the signal to let out positive particles and keep the signal brief.

Mind the Gap

No two neurons ever touch because there is a tiny gap between them called a synapse. When a nerve signal reaches a nerve end, tiny droplets of chemicals called neurotransmitters are released into the synapse. These chemicals lock onto matching receptor sites on the neighboring cell, starting a new signal.

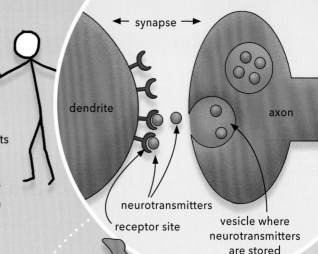

synapse

dendrite

axon

neurotransmitters

receptor site

vesicle where neurotransmitters are stored

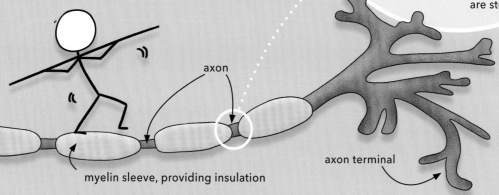

axon

myelin sleeve, providing insulation

axon terminal

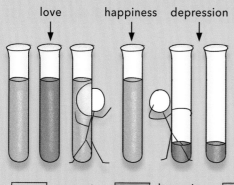

love   happiness   depression

serotonin   dopamine   oxytocin

Mood Makers

Different combinations of neurotransmitters have different effects on your mood. Having lots a neurotransmitter called serotonin puts you in a good mood. Combine it with a lot of dopamine and oxytocin, and you're in love. The less serotonin and dopamine you have, the worse your mood.

Love It

When people first fall in love, their brains flood with dopamine, which makes them feel excited, energetic, and focused—perfect for dancing or talking all night!
If the couple stays together and becomes affectionate, they get lots of oxytocin too. This is triggered when you cuddle.

Brainy

Inside your head is an amazing computer: your brain. It is made from over 100 billion neurons, each connected to 10,000–20,000 other neurons. That means there are an incredible number of connections to help you think. No wonder you're so smart!

In Your Head

Your brain fills the inside of the top of your skull. The wrinkled outer layers are known as gray matter, which is made of the bodies of nerve cells, along with dendrites and synapses. The inside of the brain is mostly white matter, which is made of axons, the long tails of nerve cells.

If you're a girl, your brain weighs 2.5 percent of your body weight, on average. If you're a boy, it weighs 2 percent—but boys' brains are heavier on average.

A Brain of Two Halves

Your brain is divided into two halves or hemispheres, linked by a huge bundle of nerves called the corpus callosum. Surprisingly, the left half of your brain controls the right side of your body, and the right half controls your left side. Each side of your brain was once thought to have very different skills (*shown below*), but many scientists now believe it is not so simple as this.

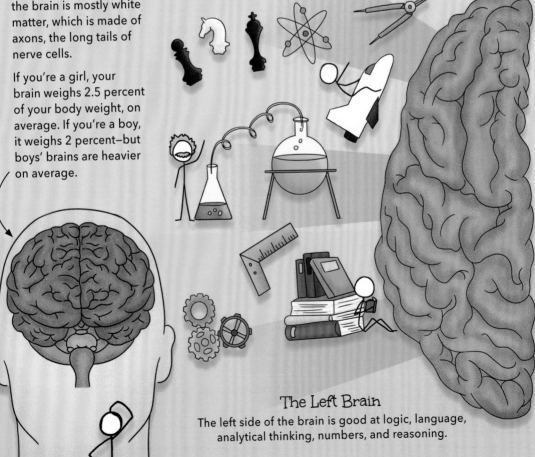

The Left Brain
The left side of the brain is good at logic, language, analytical thinking, numbers, and reasoning.

Making Up Your Mind

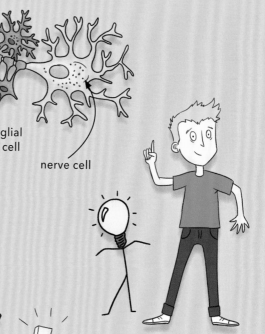

glial cell

glial cell

nerve cell

Your brain is 85 percent water. But what really matters is all the nerve cells, which are held in tight bundles by supporting cells called glial cells. All your thoughts come as signals whizzing through this amazing network.

The Right Brain

The right side of the brain is best at expressing and reading emotions, recognizing faces, intuition, and creative tasks related to music, color, and images.

There's a Thought!

Thoughts are nerve signals that buzz through the brain between nerve cells, making billions of connections in a fraction of a second. What you're thinking depends on which nerve pathways fire up. Pathways that are used a lot get stronger and quicker. Those that are not used tend to get lost.

Hungry Brain!

All those cells in your brain need a lot of energy—and a lot of oxygen! If the blood supply to your brain were cut off, you'd lose consciousness in just 10 seconds and die in minutes.

Inside Your Brain

The wrinkled outer layer of your brain is where conscious thoughts happen. Conscious thoughts are thoughts you know about. There are also subconscious thoughts occurring deep inside your brain that you know very little about!

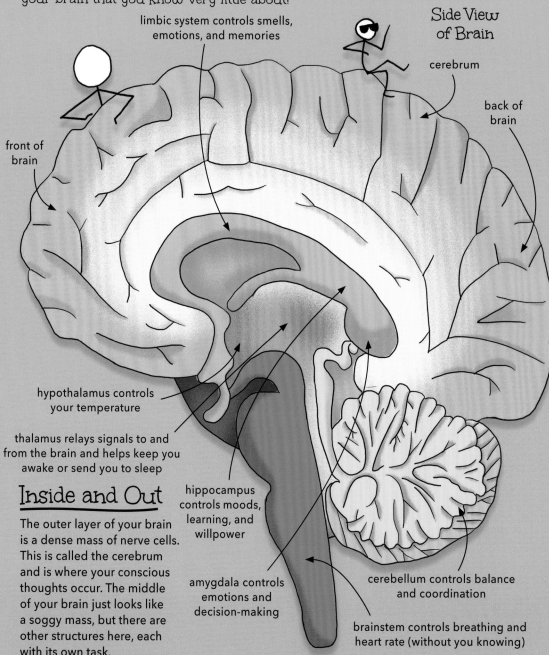

limbic system controls smells, emotions, and memories

Side View of Brain

cerebrum

front of brain

back of brain

hypothalamus controls your temperature

thalamus relays signals to and from the brain and helps keep you awake or send you to sleep

hippocampus controls moods, learning, and willpower

amygdala controls emotions and decision-making

cerebellum controls balance and coordination

brainstem controls breathing and heart rate (without you knowing)

Inside and Out

The outer layer of your brain is a dense mass of nerve cells. This is called the cerebrum and is where your conscious thoughts occur. The middle of your brain just looks like a soggy mass, but there are other structures here, each with its own task.

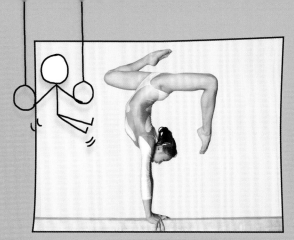

On Balance

For your body to make even a simple move, your brain has to give exact instructions to different muscles. The brain needs continual feedback from sensors in the muscles called proprioceptors, which say where every part of your body is. All these signals are coordinated in the cerebellum at the back of the brain, which then sends signals out to the correct muscles.

Brain Base

The brainstem is the stalk at the base of your brain where it runs into your spine. It's the main pathway from your brain to the rest of your body, including your face and head. The brainstem controls your breathing and heart rate and tells you when to go to sleep and when to eat.

Chess Problem

When you play chess or similar games, you use the conscious part of your brain, the cerebral cortex, to figure out the problem. But you still get better with practice as certain routines become established in your subconscious brain deep inside.

Seahorse Brain

Right in the middle of your brain is a structure shaped like a seahorse. It's called the *hippocampus*, named after the Greek for "horse" (hippo) and "sea monster" (campus). It's linked with your moods and is thought to play a key part in memory.

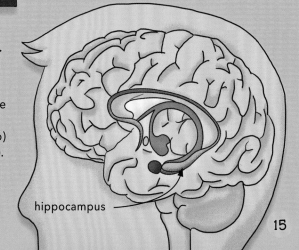

hippocampus

15

Brain Map

The cerebrum is the large, walnut-shaped bit of your brain that wraps around the inner brain like a peach around its pit. The outside of this is called the cerebral cortex. This is where all the brain's clever activities go on. It receives messages from your senses and gives commands to your muscles.

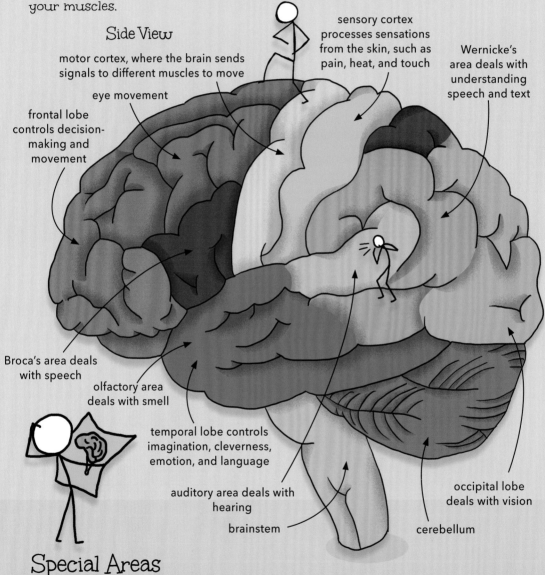

Side View

motor cortex, where the brain sends signals to different muscles to move

eye movement

frontal lobe controls decision-making and movement

sensory cortex processes sensations from the skin, such as pain, heat, and touch

Wernicke's area deals with understanding speech and text

Broca's area deals with speech

olfactory area deals with smell

temporal lobe controls imagination, cleverness, emotion, and language

auditory area deals with hearing

brainstem

occipital lobe deals with vision

cerebellum

Special Areas

Each half of your brain has four ends, called lobes. A large, very prominent one at the front, called the frontal lobe, is where all your bright ideas happen. Lots of thoughts seem to take up the whole brain. Yet certain places in the brain, called association areas, seem to become especially active when you're doing certain things.

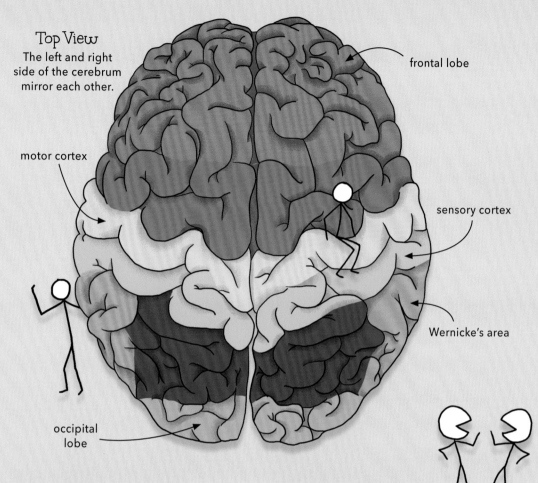

Top View
The left and right side of the cerebrum mirror each other.

frontal lobe

motor cortex

sensory cortex

Wernicke's area

occipital lobe

The Meaning Spot

When you're reading, an area near the back of the brain called Wernicke's area seems to get excited. Wernicke's area seems to be the area where you work out what you're reading and where you decide what you're going to say. This area sends instructions to Broca's area to figure out how to say it.

Chatter Spot

When you speak, an area of the brain called Broca's area seems to be involved. Scientists are not quite sure how it works. They used to think that its role was just to put words together into sentences. Now they think it may help you understand what someone else is saying too.

Moving and Feeling

There are two kinds of nerve that branch throughout your body away from your spine. Motor neurons trigger muscles to make your body move. Sensory neurons send signals from your senses to your brain to tell it what's going on.

Motor and sensory nerves are involved in whatever you're doing, whether it's writing a letter or playing football. Here's what happens when you're holding a pen:

1   Sensors in the tips of your finger and thumb trigger signals in the sensory nerve.

2   The signal travels to your spine and up to your brain.

3   In the brain, the signal is registered in the sensory cortex, a band running round the top of the brain, a bit like the strap on a set of headphones.

4   The brain responds in the neighboring motor cortex to send out a signal.

5   The signal travels through the motor neuron back down through your spine.

6   The motor neuron triggers muscles in your hand to move your finger and thumb.

Feedback

Whenever you're doing something, such as playing electronic games, there is a nonstop interaction between sensory and motor nerves. The sensory nerves continually take in data from the screen and from the world around you. The motor nerves in your hands control the screen.

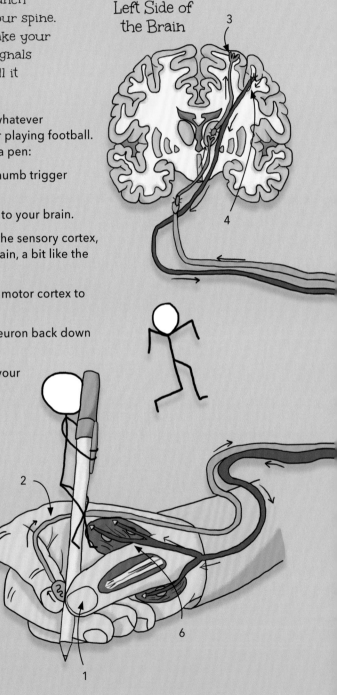

Left Side of the Brain

A Pain in the Elbow

Whenever you suffer a sharp pain, such as hitting your elbow, pain receptors send an alarm signal to your brain. You experience this alarm signal as pain, which is telling your body not to ignore the damage.

Reflexes

Reflexes are automatic reactions in your body over which you have no control. A reflex gives your body a way to respond to emergencies at lightning speed—before the danger signal has even reached your brain. It works like this:

a   You accidentally put your finger in a candle flame.

b   The sensory nerve from your finger sends a signal to your spine.

c   When the signal reaches your spine, it not only travels on to your brain, it also crosses through a link called an interneuron to the motor neuron.

d   The interneuron fires a signal down the motor neuron.

e   The motor neuron triggers the muscles in your arm to jerk your finger away from the flame.

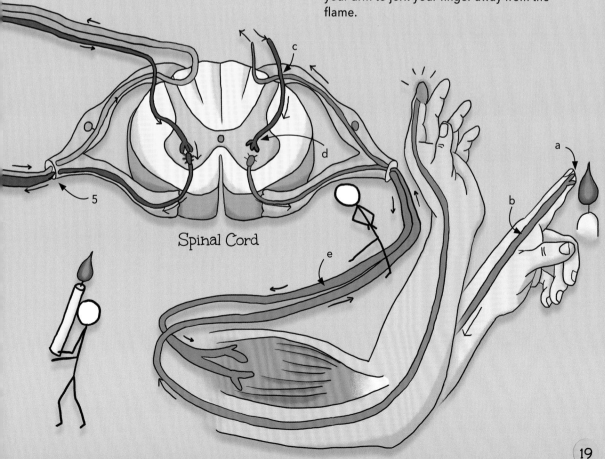

Spinal Cord

Seeing Things

Each of your eyes is an amazing camera with a powerful built-in lens that gives you an extraordinarily clear picture of the world. And behind your eyes, your brain has a visual processing system to make instant sense of the picture.

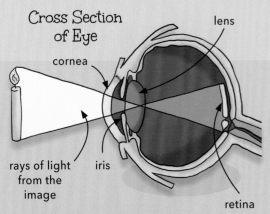

Cross Section of Eye
- lens
- cornea
- rays of light from the image
- iris
- retina

Red indicates left half of the scene. Blue indicates right half of the scene.

Making a Picture

Light from a scene you're looking at enters your eyes through the cornea, the main lens in the eye. This focuses the light to create a picture. The light then shines through a smaller lens that adjusts the focus to give a sharp picture, whether you are looking close-up or far away. The picture is upside down, but that doesn't bother your brain.

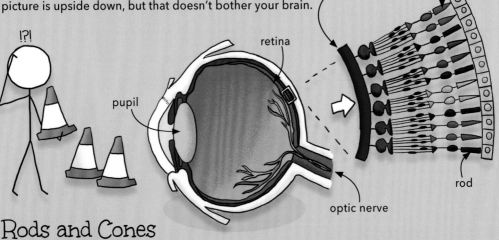

!?!

- pupil
- retina
- optic nerve
- detail of retina
- cone
- rod

Rods and Cones

The lenses project the picture onto the back of the eye, known as the retina. Here, there are two kinds of light-sensitive cell to record the picture. There are 150 million rods that detect if it's dark or light, and they work even in very low light. There are eight million cones that identify colors. These work best in daylight.

Light or Dark

Between the lenses, light passes through the pupil, the dark circle in the center of your eyes. It looks black because your eye is dark inside. The colored fringe around the pupil is the iris. In bright light, tiny muscles in the iris constrict the pupil, making it small. In dim light, the iris opens the pupil wider to let in more light.

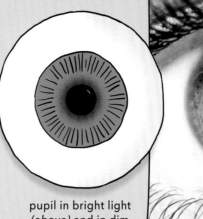
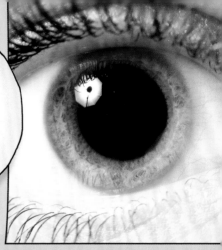

pupil in bright light *(above)* and in dim light *(right)*

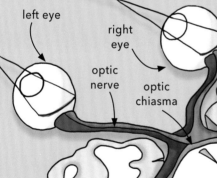

direction of light traveling to your eyes

Your Seeing Brain

From the retina, signals zoom off into your brain down the optic nerve. The optic nerves from both eyes meet and cross at the optic chiasma. Here, the signals split: half from each eye go right and half go left. Then they travel to a sorting office called the LGN. The LGN analyzes what kind of picture you're seeing—moving, dark, light, and so on. It sends each aspect of the picture to the correct place in your brain to be interpreted. Finally, your brain sees the pictures, right side up, on the screens of its own cinema, the visual cortex.

left eye

right eye

optic nerve

optic chiasma

right LGN

Red indicates left half of what you see.

left LGN

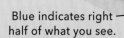

Blue indicates right half of what you see.

visual cortex

Hear, Hear

Sounds are just vibrations in the air, and your ears are clever devices for picking up these vibrations. The flaps of skin on the sides of your head that you call ears are just the entrance. The ears funnel sounds in to supersensitive detectors deep inside your brain.

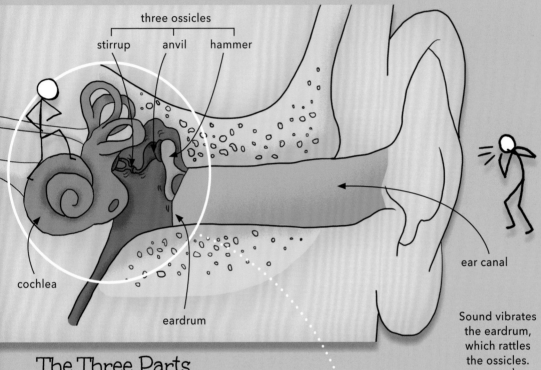

three ossicles

stirrup   anvil   hammer

cochlea

eardrum

ear canal

Sound vibrates the eardrum, which rattles the ossicles.

The Three Parts of Your Ears

The earflap and funnel into your head is the outer ear. Inside your head is the middle ear, where sound hits a wall of skin called the eardrum, shaking it rapidly. As the eardrum shakes, it rattles three tiny bones, or ossicles. These in turn tap on a window in a curly, fluid-filled tube called the cochlea, which makes up the inner ear. The rattling creates waves in the cochlea fluid, which wiggle tiny hairs so that they send signals to the brain.

The vibrations from the ossicles create waves in the cochlea that are detected by special hairs.

The ossicles make the vibrations shorter but more powerful.

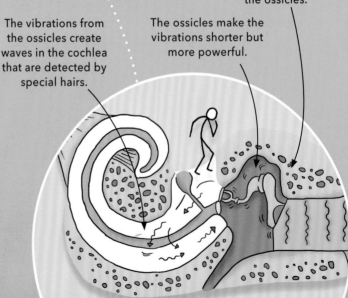

Loud or Soft?

Some sounds are loud. Some are very quiet. Loudness can be measured in decibels (dB), the force of sound waves against the ear. The louder the sound, the more decibels it is.

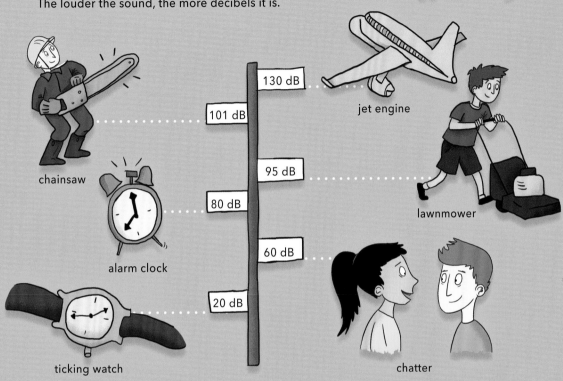

130 dB — jet engine

101 dB — chainsaw

95 dB — lawnmower

80 dB — alarm clock

60 dB — chatter

20 dB — ticking watch

Two Ears

There's a reason you have two ears. It helps you pinpoint the distance and direction of sounds. Ears are so sensitive that they can hear the very slight difference in the time that sounds take to reach each one. Your brain analyzes the difference and tells you where the sound is coming from. Some headphones fool the brain into thinking sounds really are coming from different places.

Smell That, Taste That

Your nose may not be as sensitive as a dog's, but it can identify more than three thousand different chemicals from their vapor alone. And it can detect just a few tiny particles from among billions in the air. And by working with smell, your taste is pretty sensitive too.

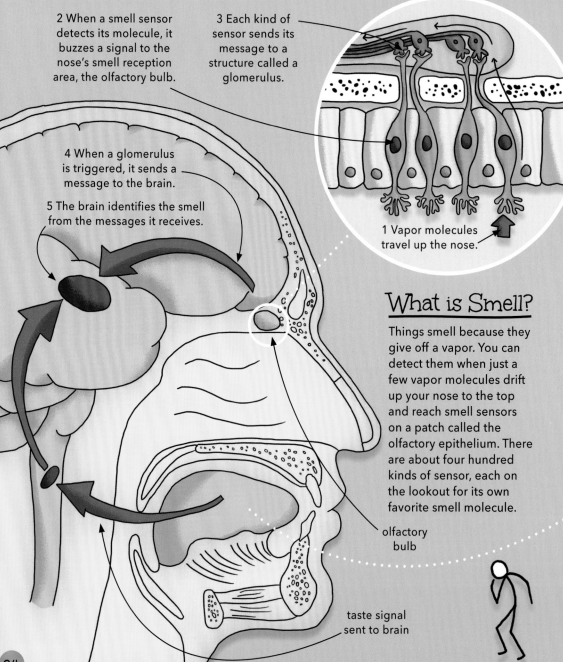

2 When a smell sensor detects its molecule, it buzzes a signal to the nose's smell reception area, the olfactory bulb.

3 Each kind of sensor sends its message to a structure called a glomerulus.

4 When a glomerulus is triggered, it sends a message to the brain.

5 The brain identifies the smell from the messages it receives.

1 Vapor molecules travel up the nose.

What is Smell?

Things smell because they give off a vapor. You can detect them when just a few vapor molecules drift up your nose to the top and reach smell sensors on a patch called the olfactory epithelium. There are about four hundred kinds of sensor, each on the lookout for its own favorite smell molecule.

olfactory bulb

taste signal sent to brain

What is Taste?

Your tongue's chemical receptors are called taste buds. There are ten thousand, located in tiny pits all over your tongue. The tiny bumps or papillae on your tongue show where they are. There are five kinds of taste bud, each sensitive to a different flavor. There are taste buds for salty, sweet, sour, and bitter tastes. There are also buds for a savory taste called umami, which is the strong taste you get from meaty dishes and soy sauce. People once thought the taste buds for each taste were in different parts of the tongue, but now it seems they are all evenly spread around.

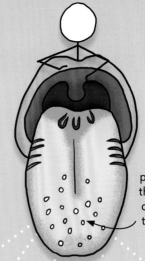

papillae on the tongue, containing taste buds

6 In each taste bud there is a cluster of cells with tiny hairs on the end.

bitter   salty   sweet   umami   sour

7 Saliva containing the food taste washes over these hairs.

8 If the taste is right for the bud, the hairs trigger sensor cells beneath to send a signal.

Dog on the Scent

If you ever catch a bad smell, be thankful you don't have a dog's sense of smell. A dog has over fifty times as many smell receptors as humans, and an olfactory area in its brain forty times as large (in proportion to its brain). That means a dog's nose is up to ten million times as sensitive as yours!

Remember, Remember

If anyone tells you you're forgetful, they're wrong! The human brain has a fantastic ability to remember. There are billions of neurons in your brain, each connecting with thousands of others. When you remember something, your brain makes a new pathway of nerve connections, called a memory trace. You forget only when connections weaken through lack of use.

Will it Last?

Memories are stored in your brain in three stages:

1   In sensory memory, new data arrives through your senses, and your senses go on seeing, hearing, or feeling something momentarily.

2   In short-term memory, the brain stores data just long enough to pass it on—like remembering a phone number while you key it in.

3   In long-term memory, your brain makes strong connections so you remember things for a long time.

Get It Into Your Head

Your brain stores long-term memories in two ways. Explicit memories are tucked away in your head quickly, and you only need to experience them a few times to remember them. But implicit memories only stick when you go over them again and again, as when you learn to play the piano or football. These memories are stored by making nerve connections throughout your body, not just in your brain.

What a Moment!

Some memories are episodic. These are dramatic episodes, such as a memorable Christmas. You remember every sensation and may be able to recall them years later.

It's a Fact

Facts such as the tallest mountain (Mount Everest) are called semantic memories. Your brain seems to store these in the temporal lobe in the left of your brain.

Practice Makes Perfect

You teach your body skills and procedures, such as playing a musical instrument, by practicing them, so that the correct nerve connections are slowly built up.

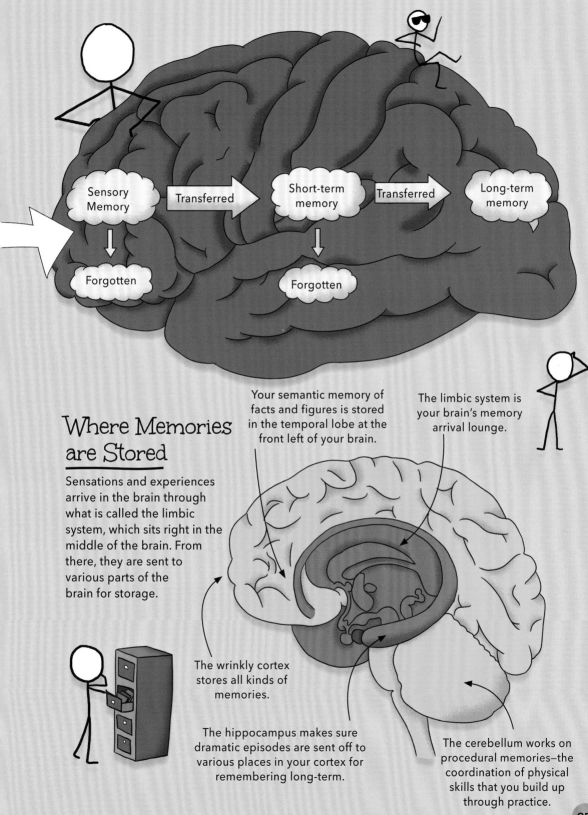

Sensory Memory

Transferred

Short-term memory

Transferred

Long-term memory

Forgotten

Forgotten

Where Memories are Stored

Sensations and experiences arrive in the brain through what is called the limbic system, which sits right in the middle of the brain. From there, they are sent to various parts of the brain for storage.

Your semantic memory of facts and figures is stored in the temporal lobe at the front left of your brain.

The limbic system is your brain's memory arrival lounge.

The wrinkly cortex stores all kinds of memories.

The hippocampus makes sure dramatic episodes are sent off to various places in your cortex for remembering long-term.

The cerebellum works on procedural memories—the coordination of physical skills that you build up through practice.

The History of the Brain

For a long time, scientists knew surprisingly little about the brain and nerves. They weren't even sure that the brain does your thinking. But discoveries about electricity and the development of microscopes led to many breakthroughs. Knowing about electricity helped scientists understand how nerves work. Microscopes helped them see actual nerves for the first time.

450 BCE

The Ancient Greek thinker Alcmaeon was one of the first to realize that the brain is where your thoughts occur. Most people at the time believed thoughts happened in your heart.

1871

A young Italian anatomist named Camillo Golgi figured out how to see nerve cells clearly by staining them with silver nitrate. He saw that they have a single long axon and spindly dendrites that spread out from the spiderlike cell body.

200 BCE	1400	1600

200 CE

The Roman doctor Galen believed that muscles were controlled by the lower, tougher part of the brain, the cerebellum, whereas the softer top of the brain controlled the senses. He was not entirely wrong—the cerebellum does coordinate muscles.

1630

The French thinker René Descartes believed that the mind interacted with the brain through a point in the center of the brain called the pineal gland.

1780

The Italian scientist Luigi Galvani conducted famous experiments to make frogs' legs twitch by wiring them up to batteries. He concluded, partially correctly, that nerves work electrically.

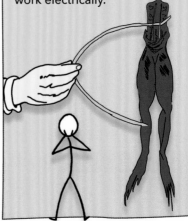

1890

The Spanish neuroscientist Santiago Ramón y Cajal discovered that nerve cells don't touch directly. Instead they pass on signals across narrow gaps called synapses.

1906

The British neuroscientist Charles Sherrington showed that the nervous system is not one big single circuit, like an electrical circuit. It is lots of separate nerve cells working in balance.

1940s

The American scientists Edgar Adrian, Herbert Gasser, and Joseph Erlanger showed that the electricity in a nerve is not like an electric current. Instead it sweeps along the nerve as an action potential—a difference in electrical charge between the inside of the nerve and the outside.

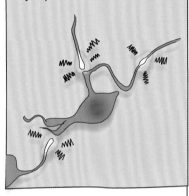

1800 **1900** **2000**

1950

The American psychologist Karl Spencer Lashley experimented by testing how rats found their way through mazes with various bits of the brain removed. He concluded that memories are not stored in one place in the brain, but all throughout it.

1990s

The Swedish brain drug specialist Arvid Carlsson found that people with Parkinson's disease had low levels of the neurotransmitter dopamine. This led to the development of L-DOPA, a drug for treating the disease.

1950s

The German scientist Bernard Katz and Austrian refugee Stephen Kuffler discovered that nerve signals are sent on to the next nerve across the synapse by means of special chemicals called neurotransmitters.

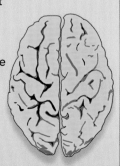

2001

The American neuroscientist Elkhonon Goldberg realized that brain activity is all coordinated by the brain's command center right at the front, called the prefrontal cortex.

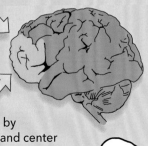

More Brainy Facts

Baby Brain

Your brain grows at an amazing rate before you're born. At times, a quarter of a million neurons can be added every minute! But as soon as you're born, neurons stop growing, and you have all the neurons you'll ever have.

Brain Pruning

In fact, as you grow older, you lose more and more neurons in a process called apoptosis. That doesn't mean you become less smart. It's actually a necessary process of streamlining, as unneeded neurons are weeded out. And the number of connections between neurons, the real key to cleverness, goes on growing and growing.

Growing Brain

Even though you gain no more neurons after you're born, your brain continues to grow. By the time you're two, it's still only 80 percent of its adult size. So how is that? The answer is that the glial cells, the supporting cells around the neurons, continue to grow. Glial cells seem to protect your neurons and help them work better.

Mirror Neurons

A few decades ago, scientists discovered that neurons don't fire just when you do something. Some neurons fire when someone else does something. These neurons are called mirror neurons. When you see a soccer player weaving her way to the goal, you feel involved because your own mirror neurons give you the same twisting and turning sensation.

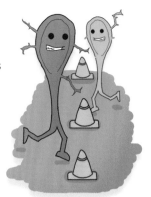

Hot Head

Thinking is hard work. Your brain uses a lot of energy, more than any other part of the body. It uses more than 20 percent of all your energy by itself. The brain runs on about 12 watts of power—about a fifth of the average electric light bulb.

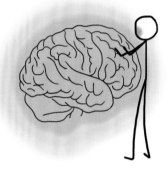

A Brain like Einstein

Girls' brains are slightly smaller than boys' brains, but it doesn't make them any less clever. The great scientist Albert Einstein had a smaller brain than average, yet he is thought to be one of the smartest people ever.

Waste of Space

Some people say you use only 10 percent of your brain at any one time. A recent Hollywood movie was based on the idea that if you learned to use your whole brain, you would gain superpowers. But that's a myth. The entire brain is already active all of the time, even when you're asleep.

INDEX

autonomic nervous
   system, 9

brainstem, 14–15
Broca's area, 17

central nervous system, 8
cerebellum, 15, 28
cerebral cortex, 15–16
cerebrum, 14, 16

ears, 22–23
Einstein, Albert, 31
eyes, 20–21

feeling, 18–19, 26

hippocampus, 15

Intelligence Quotient (IQ),
   6

memory, 15, 26–27
mirror neurons, 31
motor neurons, 18

nervous system, 6, 8–10, 29
neurons, 10–12, 18–19, 26,
   30–31
neurotransmitters, 11, 29

pain, 9, 19
peripheral nervous
   system, 8

reflexes, 19

sciatic nerve, 9
sight, 20–21
smell, 24–25
sound, 22–23
spinal cord, 8–9

taste, 24–25
thoughts, 7, 13–14,
   16, 28

vagus nerve, 9

Wernicke's area, 17

The Author

John Farndon is Royal Literary Fellow at City&Guilds in London, United Kingdom, and the author of a huge number of books for adults and children on science, technology, and nature, including such international best sellers as *Do Not Open* and *Do You Think You're Clever?*. He has been shortlisted six times for the Royal Society's Young People's Book Prize for a science book, with titles such as *How the Earth Works, What Happens When?*, and *Project Body* (2016).

The Illustrator

Venitia Dean is a freelance illustrator who grew up in Brighton, United Kingdom. She has loved drawing ever since she could hold a pencil! As a teenager she discovered a passion for figurative illustration, and when she turned nineteen she was given a digital drawing tablet for her birthday and started transferring her work to the computer. She hasn't looked back since! As well as illustration, Venitia loves reading graphic novels and walking her dog Peanut.

Picture Credits (abbreviations: t = top; b = bottom; c = center; l = left; r = right)
© www.shutterstock.com:

6 tl, 6 br, 7 tl, 7 cr, 7 bl, 15 tl, 21 tr, 26 bl, 26 bc, 26 br,
7 bl = Tony Baggett / Shutterstock.com